A TASTE OF ITALY

Jenny Ridgwell

Wayland

Titles in this series

A TASTE OF

Britain   India
China   Italy
France   Japan

Cover *Sunflowers growing in front of a hilltop village in Tuscany, northern Italy.*

Frontispiece *Sweet red peppers were brought to Italy from America in the sixteenth century. They are now an important ingredient in Italian cooking.*

Editor: Anna Girling
Designer: Jean Wheeler

First published in 1993 by
Wayland (Publishers) Ltd
61 Western Road, Hove
East Sussex, BN3 1JD, England

British Library Cataloguing in Publication Data
Ridgwell, Jenny
Taste of Italy. – (Food Around the
World Series)
I. Title II. Series
641.5945

ISBN 0 7502 0744 2

Typeset by Dorchester Typesetting Group Ltd
Printed and bound by Lego, Italy

Contents

Italy – its farming and food

Above *Rome is a busy, crowded city.* Below *Grapevines in northern Italy, with mountains in the background. Much of Italy is mountainous.*

Italy is a long, narrow country sticking out from Europe into the Mediterranean Sea. It is 1,200 km long from north to south. In shape, it looks rather like a boot. In the north, Italy is separated from the rest of Europe by the high mountains of the Alps. Two large Mediterranean islands, Sicily and Sardinia, are also part of Italy.

Italy is one of the most crowded countries in Europe. It has a population of about 58 million people, most of whom live in the cities and towns. Rome is the capital city.

Farming

In the past many Italians were farmers. Over the last fifty years, however, Italian industry has grown quickly. Nowadays, more people work in industry than in farming.

Much of the land is mountainous, which makes farming difficult in these areas. However, Italy still manages to produce a lot of food. The main crops are grapes, wheat and olives.

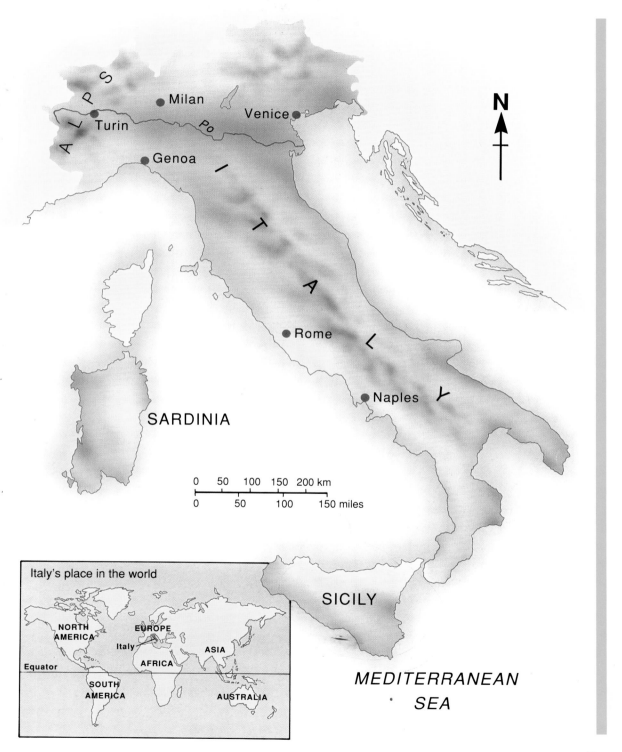

N

ALPS
Milan
Turin
Po
Venice
Genoa
ITALY
Rome
Naples
SARDINIA

0 50 100 150 200 km
0 50 100 150 miles

Italy's place in the world

NORTH
AMERICA
EUROPE
Italy
ASIA
AFRICA
Equator
SOUTH
AMERICA
AUSTRALIA

SICILY

*MEDITERRANEAN
SEA*

A taste of Italy

Wheat and wine are important crops. This picture shows rolling wheat fields as well as vines.

The hills of southern Italy are covered with groves of olive trees.

Italy is famous for its wine (made from grapes) and is the second largest producer of olive oil in the world. It is also the second largest wheat producer in Europe. Two types of wheat are grown: hard wheat for making pasta and soft wheat for making bread.

Other important crops include rice, maize and citrus fruits such as lemons and oranges.

Cattle, sheep and goats are reared for their meat and for milk. Milk is used to make butter and cheese. Pigs are also important because Italy produces a lot of ham and *salami*, made from pork.

Climate

Because of Italy's long shape, there is a big difference in climate between northern and southern areas. This has an effect on the farming and cooking in the different regions.

In the cooler north of Italy there is rich farmland for growing cereal crops. The north also has plenty of grazing land for cattle, which are used to produce milk. People in the north use a lot of butter, cheese and milk in their cooking.

In the hot south there are many olive groves and vineyards. People also grow salad vegetables, such as tomatoes and peppers. In southern regions, people use olive oil instead of butter for cooking and they eat delicious salads.

The mountains of northern Italy provide grazing for cattle.

Peppers, onions and tomatoes are important ingredients in southern Italy.

Italian food in the past

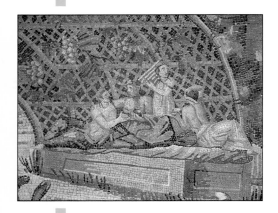

The ancient Romans enjoyed lavish feasts. They lay down on long seats to eat and were served by slaves.

Food in Roman times

Over 2,000 years ago the ancient Romans ruled Italy. It seems that they were very good cooks. Many of today's Italian foods, such as wild boar and songbirds, can be traced back to Roman times. Rich people ate huge amounts of expensive foods. Writers from Roman times tell of tables laden with cooked peacocks, flamingos and herons. Dormice were another favourite Roman food. The dormice were kept and fattened up in special barrels.

Songbirds are still a popular food in Italy today. This dish of roast thrush comes from Sardinia.

The Romans divided their large meals into three parts. This habit was copied by other Europeans and still exists today. The *antipasto* course was eaten first to make the eater feel hungry. *Antipasto* is Italian for 'before the meal'. The main part of the meal was meat, fish and vegetables. Finally, there was a dish of sweet foods, such as grapes and dates.

The Romans learnt how to make salt from sea water. Salt is a very important ingredient. It is useful for seasoning and preserving food. The Romans became wealthy from selling salt to other parts of the world.

It must be remembered, however, that most ordinary Romans ate quite a poor diet. A meal was often thick porridge followed by coarse bread with olives, beans, figs and cheese.

The Middle Ages

During the Middle Ages, Arabs from northern Africa settled in southern Italy and Sicily. They brought with them the art of making sweets from honey and nuts.

Spices from Asia were also introduced and imported through Genoa and Venice. Italians learnt to use these new spices in their cooking. Saffron, for example, was and still is used in *risotto*.

Risotto *made with saffron. The saffron gives the rice a strong, yellow colour.*

A taste of Italy

Above *Hot peppers are dried in the air.* Below *Italian plum tomatoes are long and thin, not round.*

Foods from America

In the fifteenth century European explorers reached America for the first time. Over the years, sailors brought back foods from America that had never been seen in Europe. These included tomatoes, potatoes, maize and sweet peppers.

The first tomatoes brought to Italy from South America were yellow. Later, however, people discovered that red tomatoes grew well in the warm Italian climate. Today, both fresh and canned Italian tomatoes are sold to many parts of the world.

Polenta, *made from maize, is often served with stews.*

Potatoes were brought from Peru. At first they were grown in Italian gardens as decorative plants. Later, people discovered they were good to eat, too.

Maize was first brought to Italy in about 1650. It was made into a thick, yellow porridge, called *polenta. Polenta* soon became a popular food in Italy. It is still served today, with meat stews or mixed with butter and cheese.

Italian food around the world

Over the years, many people from the southern regions of Italy have left to live in other countries, such as the United States, Canada and Australia. These settlers have often set up Italian food shops and restaurants in their new countries. Today, Italian food is popular in many countries of the world.

The Italian way of life

Italians love to sit at cafés and chat with friends over a cup of coffee.

Family, friends and food play an important part in Italian life. Families meet regularly for meals and celebrations. In many towns people go for an evening stroll around the streets and friends gather for coffee and ice-cream in cafés and bars.

Everyday eating

Italians eat bread with every meal. In many families, the first job of the day is to go out to a baker's shop to buy some fresh bread.

Breakfast is usually a quick snack of milky coffee or hot drinking chocolate, with sweet rolls or *croissants*.

Bread stalls sell fresh bread every day.

Lunch is a time for the whole family to get together for a meal.

Many Italians have a long lunch break of about two hours. Shops and offices close and families often go home to eat. Some schoolchildren may take a packed lunch from home if their school is a long way away.

The main meal of the day is in the evening and is eaten at about 7 pm. It might consist of vegetable soup, bread, meat and salad, followed by fruit.

13

Above *Italians tend to prefer shopping at small grocery shops rather than at supermarkets.*

Market day in Padua, a large city in northern Italy.

Shopping

In general, Italians like to buy fresh food each day from small local shops. As a result, Italy has more small grocery shops than any other country in Europe. In recent years, large superstores have opened on the outskirts of towns and cities. However, compared to other countries, these are few in number.

Most towns have a special market day once a week, when stalls are set up in a square in the town centre. These markets are always busy places, with stalls selling fresh fruit, vegetables, cheeses and meat.

Cooking

Italians like to eat good quality food prepared using traditional methods. Italian cooks tend to use simple, basic equipment rather than modern machines and gadgets.

For example, only 4 per cent of homes in Italy have a microwave cooker. In the United Kingdom the figure is 48 per cent. Only 28 per cent of Italian homes have a freezer, compared with 87 per cent in Norway and Sweden.

Is the Italian diet healthy?

Scientists have studied what they call the 'Mediterranean diet'. This is the type of food generally eaten by people in the Mediterranean region – including the Italians. The Mediterranean diet consists of plenty of starchy foods, such as bread, pasta and potatoes, lots of fresh fruit and vegetables, olive oil and fish. And a little wine sometimes!

Scientists have discovered that people who eat a Mediterranean diet are less likely to suffer from heart disease. They also do not suffer greatly from food-related illnesses such as constipation and diabetes. Food experts suggest that people should copy this way of eating in order to stay healthy.

This chart shows the different types of food eaten, per person, in Italy and the United Kingdom each year.

You can see that the Italians eat much more starchy food, such as flour and potatoes, and less fat from milk and butter than people in the United Kingdom. They eat less sugar too.

	Italy kg	United Kingdom kg
flour	115	83
potatoes	141	108
meat	89	78
milk	75	128
butter	2	5
sugar	2	5

Pasta

Twists, tubes, shells and bows – these are just some of the hundreds of different shapes of pasta.

There are said to be 200 different shapes of pasta – and over 600 different names for the shapes! Italian pasta dishes have become popular all over the world.

No one knows when the Italians started to eat pasta. One popular story is that the Italian explorer Marco Polo, who travelled to Asia in the thirteenth century, brought back the recipe from China. In China people eat egg noodles, which are similar to pasta. It seems, though, that people in Europe have been eating some form of pasta for several thousand years.

The word 'pasta' means paste or dough in Italian. Pasta is made from a special hard wheat, called durum wheat, which is mixed with water, and sometimes milk or eggs, to form a dough.

Over the years the Italians have invented many different shapes and sizes of pasta. Shapes are made by pressing the dough into moulds to make shells or spirals, or by squeezing it out to make lengths for *vermicelli*, *macaroni* or *spaghetti*.

Pasta is made from very simple ingredients – flour, water and, sometimes, eggs.

Many Italians use pasta machines. The dough is put in at the back of the machine and is squeezed out through metal 'teeth' to make flat noodles, spaghetti *or* macaroni.

A taste of Italy

Red, black, green and brown pasta.

The pasta can be used fresh, straightaway, or dried and kept for later. Either way, it is cooked by boiling it in water for several minutes until it is soft but chewy.

Pasta can be made in different colours and flavours by adding other ingredients. For example, green spinach, red tomatoes or black squid ink can be mixed into the dough. People have even made chocolate-flavoured pasta!

Make your own pasta

In Italy people use special machines to make pasta at home. The dough is squeezed through holes to make thin, flat noodles or round lengths of *spaghetti* or *macaroni*. This is an easy recipe for making pasta by hand.

Ingredients
Serves 2

100 g strong plain white flour
pinch of salt
1 teaspoon cooking oil
1 beaten egg
2 teaspoons water

Equipment

bowl
rolling pin
knife
large saucepan
sieve

1 Put all the ingredients in a bowl and mix with your hands to make a dough. Squeeze and knead it for 2-3 minutes until it is smooth.

2   Sprinkle some flour on to a work top and roll out the dough very thinly.

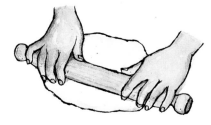

3   Cut it into strips or invent your own shapes.

4   Cook for 3-5 minutes in a large saucepan of boiling water. The pasta should be soft but still firm and chewy.

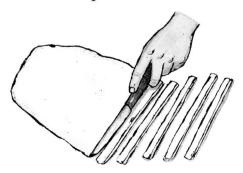

5   Drain through a sieve over the sink. Serve hot with tomato sauce or *pesto* (basil sauce). You can buy ready-made sauces in jars from supermarkets.

Always be careful with boiling water. Ask an adult to help you.

A simple dish of pasta with pesto sauce.

Meat and fish

Meat, poultry and game

As well as the usual animals eaten for meat – beef cattle, sheep, pigs and chickens – Italians also enjoy eating animals caught for sport. This meat is called game, and includes rabbit, wild boar and small birds.

Italy is famous for some of its meat products, such as hams and sausages.

Parma ham is a dark red colour.

Parma ham

Ham is made from the back leg of a pig, which is treated with salt. This process is called 'curing'. In years gone by, ham-making was a way of preserving the meat to make it last through the winter.

Parma ham is the best-known Italian ham. It is cured, then left for a year before it is eaten. This long process makes Parma ham expensive to buy. It is cut into very thin slices and people only eat a little at a time!

Salami

Salami are spicy sausages which were invented in Italy. Now, however, many other countries have copied the recipe. *Salami* are made from chopped meat mixed with salt and spices, such as pepper, paprika and garlic. The sausages are then dried in the air or smoked.

Many different types of salami *are made in Italy.*

Fish and seafood are best eaten very fresh. These harbourside stalls sell fish straight from the fishing boats.

Fish

Italians eat a huge variety of sea fish, such as tuna fish, hake, sardines and anchovies. They also eat other seafood, such as lobsters, shrimps, mussels, squid and octopus, and freshwater fish, including trout.

Fishing is an important industry in Italy, particularly in Sicily and Sardinia. However, over the years the Mediterranean has become more and more polluted. Now the fishing boats travel further for their catches – even as far as the Atlantic Ocean.

Cheese

The ancient Romans made at least thirteen different cheeses. Some of their recipes are still used today. The Italians make cheese from milk from cows, sheep, goats and even buffaloes.

Parmesan
Parmesan (or *Parmegiano reggiano*) is the cheese grated over pasta. It is made in northern Italy. As much as 16 kg of milk is used to make just 1 kg of cheese. The cheese is then left for two years. Parmesan is hard and salty. It will keep for several years.

Above *The Italians produce a wide variety of hard and soft cheeses.*
Right *Buffaloes are kept for their milk, which is used to make* mozzarella.

Mozzarella

Soft, white *mozzarella* is the cheese used as a *pizza* topping. When cooked, it stretches into long strands. The best *mozzarella* is made from buffaloes' milk. Today, however, Italy has few buffaloes, so cows' milk is used instead. Fresh *mozzarella* is kept in whey and should be eaten soon after it is made.

Gorgonzola

The famous blue cheese, *Gorgonzola*, comes from the north of Italy. It has a strong smell and tangy taste. To make *Gorgonzola*, copper wires are inserted into the cheese. This helps the mould that produces the blue colour to grow.

Mozzarella *and tomato salad is a delicious Italian starter.*

Other important ingredients

Olives

Olives are eaten as a snack or made into olive oil.

Olives are an important crop in central and southern Italy, where olive trees grow all over the hillsides. In the autumn, when the olives are ready for picking, farmers place nets under the trees and knock off the olives with sticks. Green olives are ones that have been picked before they have ripened. Black olives have been allowed to ripen fully before picking.

Both black and green olives are too bitter to be eaten straight from the tree. They have to be soaked in salt water before they are ready to eat.

Whole olives, stones and all, are crushed to make olive oil. Oil from the first pressing is called 'extra virgin'. It is strong-tasting and expensive. The olives are then pressed again several times to produce cheaper, but milder, oils.

At harvest time, farmers spread nets under their olive trees to catch the falling fruit.

Olives change from green to black as they ripen.

Rice

Rice is the main ingredient in *risotto*, a dish from northern Italy. A special, very expensive, rice, called *arborio*, is used. When cooked, this rice becomes creamy on the outside, while staying crunchy in the middle.

Arborio rice is grown in the valley of the River Po. Rice needs plenty of water and warmth to grow, so the land is flooded. It then has to be drained before harvesting.

Rice fields are flooded with water before the rice seedlings are planted out.

25

A taste of Italy

Bread is made in different shapes and flavours. Nuts and seeds are often added.

Wild mushrooms are a favourite food. Many different varieties are eaten.

Bread

The ancient Romans ate a range of different breads, both sweet and savoury. To the basic flour dough, they added other ingredients, such as honey, oil, wine and milk. The Romans ate their bread with meat or dipped it into goats' milk or wine as a quick snack.

Today, Italians eat delicious fresh bread with nearly every meal. Bread is made with white or wholemeal flour and there are many varieties and shapes from different regions. *Pagnotta* is a large, coarse country loaf, which keeps fresh for several days. *Panini* are long, soft rolls used for sandwiches.

Vegetables and fruit

Tomatoes, peppers, onions and garlic are used in many Italian dishes. Fresh herbs, such as basil, oregano and parsley, are important flavourings. Other popular vegetables in Italy include artichokes,

Sicily has an excellent climate for growing fruit and vegetables. This stall is in the Sicilian capital, Palermo.

aubergines and spinach. The Italians are also fond of all kinds of mushrooms.

Fruit is eaten at the end of a meal. The warm Italian climate is perfect for growing fruits such as grapes, peaches and figs.

Ice-cream and water ices

The ancient Romans discovered how to keep ice, even in summer, and made ices from frozen, sweetened water. They thought of freezing cream, too, sweetened with honey or sugar. Today, Italy is famous for its delicious ice-creams.

There are two types of Italian ices. *Gelato* is made from cream and comes in flavours such as pistachio (a kind of nut), chocolate and vanilla. *Granita* is a water ice flavoured with crushed fruits, such as strawberries or lemons.

Cassata (a mixture of ice-cream and fruit) and Neapolitan (layers of different ice-creams) are famous Italian desserts.

Italian ice-creams are often exciting mixtures of ice-cream, cream, fruit, nuts and wafers.

27

Drinks

Grapes are harvested in the late summer.

Wine

The Italians produce a great deal of wine. Grapes are grown in large vineyards. Often, groups of farmers from one area take their grapes to a central organization where the grapes are pressed and made into wine. Money made from selling the wine is shared between the farmers.

There are over 4,000 different types of bottled wine in Italy. Famous Italian wines include *Chianti* (a red wine) and *Asti spumante* (a sweet, sparkling wine).

A modern winery. Farmers from the surrounding area bring their grapes to be pressed and made into wine.

An Italian shop selling a wide range of wines and vermouths.

Italian wines are sometimes made into vermouth. This is made from wine flavoured with herbs. It is drunk before lunch or dinner.

Italians drink 'bitters' to soothe an upset stomach or indigestion. This is made from wine flavoured with herbs and flowers – and it tastes very bitter indeed!

Coffee

Coffee was introduced in Italy from Arabia, in the Middle East, many centuries ago. The first coffee shops opened in Venice. Now they are found all around the world.

Italians drink coffee throughout the day. *Cappuccino* is frothy, milky coffee topped with chocolate powder and it is drunk in the morning. Strong, black *espresso* coffee is popular after a meal.

Cappuccino coffee is made with hot, frothy milk.

29

Festival food

Most Italians are Roman Catholics. Throughout the year there are many festivals linked to religious events, such as Christmas and Easter. At these times, families celebrate with special foods.

Christmas

Christmas is the most important family festival in Italy. Some Italians eat their celebration meal on Christmas Eve (24 December) before they go to church for midnight Mass. Others have their Christmas meal on Christmas Day (25 December). The meal often lasts all day!

An Italian Christmas meal is made up of many courses. In each region of Italy, different favourite specialities are included. It is followed by Italian Christmas cake, called *panettone*. This is a light sponge cake made from candied fruit and raisins. It is served with sweet, sparkling *Asti spumante* wine.

Italian Christmas cake, panettone, *is a light sponge with dried fruit.*

Below is an example of the sort of Christmas Eve meal that might be eaten by a family from Naples, in southern Italy.

- Rich soup made with spinach
- Pasta served with a meat and tomato sauce
- Several fish dishes, including cod and eels
- *Panettone*
- Nuts and fruit

- Sliced raw vegetables and mayonnaise
- *Ravioli* (pasta squares filled with cheese and spinach)
- Roast beef with courgettes, carrots and fried potatoes
- Goats'-milk cheese
- Fruit and nuts
- Crème caramel
- *Panettone* (after a short rest!)

Above is an example of a family meal for Christmas Day in Turin, in the north of Italy.

Easter

Easter is another important festival. Most Italians eat roast lamb at Easter. In the south people make a savoury round pastry with eggs and ham. In Liguria, in north-west Italy, people make an Easter pie from thirty-three thin sheets of pastry filled with cheese, eggs and spinach. Each sheet of pastry stands for a year in the life of Jesus Christ.

Torrone, which is like nougat, is a traditional sweet eaten as a treat at all Italian festivals.

A bakery selling special Easter breads. 'Buona Pasqua' is Italian for 'Happy Easter'.

Minestrone *soup*

Ingredients
Serves 4

1 carrot, peeled and
   chopped
2 sticks celery,
   washed and
   chopped
1 small onion, peeled
   and chopped
2 rashers bacon,
   chopped
1 tablespoon
   vegetable oil
1 litre water
salt and pepper
50 g *spaghetti*
50 g small frozen peas
Parmesan cheese

Minestrone is a filling soup made from lots of vegetables, beans and pasta. Eat it with lots of crusty bread and it is a meal in itself!

Minestrone *soup can be made using all kinds of vegetables – whatever is available.*

1 Heat the carrot, celery, onion and bacon in the oil in a large saucepan. Stir all the time until the vegetables begin to soften.

2 Pour in the water, bring to the boil and season with salt and pepper. Then add the *spaghetti*, broken into small pieces. Cook for 10 minutes.

3 Add the frozen peas and cook for a further 5 minutes.

4 Ladle into large soup bowls and sprinkle on some Parmesan cheese.

Always be careful with boiling water. Ask an adult to help you.

33

Bean and tuna fish salad

This dish is quick to make and can be eaten at the start of a meal or as a main course with other salads.

Fishing for tuna near Sicily. Tuna are very large fish. Their meaty flesh is cut into steaks.

Ingredients
Serves 2–4

430 g can butter beans or kidney beans
200 g can tuna fish in brine
2 spring onions, finely chopped
black pepper
olive oil
juice of ½ lemon

Equipment

can-opener
sieve
large bowl
knife and chopping board

Bean and tuna fish salad

1   Open the cans of beans and tuna fish. Drain off the liquid.

Always be careful with knives and can-openers. Ask an adult to help you.

2   In a bowl, mix together the beans, tuna fish and spring onions. Season with pepper, a little olive oil and lemon juice.

3   Serve with lots of crusty bread.

The Italians eat all kinds of beans. Dried beans have to be soaked and cooked before eating. Canned beans are ready to eat.

Pasta with ham and leek

Ingredients
Serves 2

1 leek
2 tablespoons
   vegetable oil
100 g cooked ham, cut
   into thin strips
100 g dried pasta
   spirals
150 ml single cream
black pepper
grated Parmesan
   cheese

Equipment

knife and chopping
   board
saucepan with lid
large saucepan
sieve
wooden spoon

1 Wash the leek well and cut it into thin slices. Wash under running water to remove any soil.

2 Heat the oil in a saucepan, add the sliced leek and cook gently until it softens. Turn off the heat. Add the ham and cover with a lid.

Pasta with ham and leek

Pasta with a cream and ham sauce is a popular dish from northern Italy.

3 Cook the pasta in a large pan of boiling water, following the instructions on the packet. It should be soft but still chewy. Drain in a sieve over a sink.

Always be careful with boiling water. Ask an adult to help you.

4 Stir the cream into the leeks and ham and season with pepper.

5 Mix this sauce into the pasta and serve hot, sprinkled with Parmesan cheese.

Risotto *with sausage*

Ingredients
Serves 4

150 g skinless
    sausages
1 onion, finely
    chopped
25 g butter
200 g *risotto* or long
    grain rice
500 ml water
100 g mushrooms,
    sliced
2 large chopped
    tomatoes
salt and pepper
grated Parmesan
    cheese

All kinds of ingredients can be added to risotto. *This one is made with asparagus.*

Risotto is a creamy rice dish which comes from the north of Italy. Usually it is made with lots of butter. For this recipe you can use vegetable oil instead.

Equipment

knife and chopping
   board
saucepan with lid
heavy saucepan
wooden spoon
measuring jug
kettle

1 Cut the sausages into slices and 'dry fry' in a saucepan without any oil, stirring all the time. Add the mushrooms, tomatoes and a little water to make a sauce. Season with salt and pepper, cover with a lid and cook for 10 minutes.

2 Cook the onion in the butter in a heavy saucepan until soft. Add the rice and cook, stirring, for 1 minute.

3 Boil some water in a kettle and pour 500 ml into a heat-proof measuring jug. Add a little at a time to the rice, stirring as it cooks. Let the rice simmer for about 10 minutes until it is soft. Add more water if necessary.

Always be careful with boiling water. Ask an adult to help you.

4 When the rice is cooked, mix in the sausage mixture and serve hot, sprinkled with grated Parmesan cheese.

39

Granita di limone

Italians are famous for their water ices and ice-creams. Try this home-made recipe for lemon water ice. Remember to stir the mixture often as it freezes, so that the water ice is soft, not solid.

Try making orange, coffee and strawberry water ices.

Ingredients
Serves 6

500 ml water
125 g sugar
juice and rind of
    2 lemons

Equipment

saucepan
grater or zester
lemon squeezer
plastic tray or tub

1 Boil the water and sugar in a saucepan for 5 minutes, stirring to make sure the sugar dissolves.

Always be careful with boiling water. Ask an adult to help you.

2 Remove from the heat, add the lemon juice and grated lemon rind and leave to cool.

3 Pour into a tray or tub which can be put in a freezer. Place in the freezer for 3-4 hours.

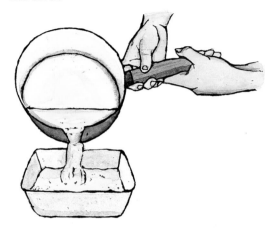

4 Stir every 30 minutes to scrape the ice crystals into the mixture. This makes a softer, finer water ice.

5 Try making other water ices flavoured with orange juice, coffee or strawberries.

Neapolitan pizza

Pizza *topped with onions and red and green peppers.*

The ancient Romans made a kind of *pizza* from bread dough, onions and oil. There was no tomato topping because tomatoes only arrived in Italy in the fifteenth century.

Pizza is now made all over the world, but it first came from Naples. It was simply bread dough topped with tomatoes and *mozzarella* cheese, baked in a hot oven.

Italian families visit a *pizzeria* to buy *pizza* ready made. This idea has been copied elsewhere. Takeaway *pizza* restaurants can now be found all over the world.

Equipment

baking tray
measuring jug
mixing bowl
rolling pin
grater
can-opener

Make your own *pizza* following this traditional recipe and add your own extra toppings.

1 Set the oven at 220°C/425°F or gas mark 7. Grease a large baking tray with a little vegetable oil.

2 Make the dough. Sprinkle the yeast and sugar into the warm water in a measuring jug and leave to froth for about 10 minutes.

This pizza *is about to be put into the oven at an Italian* pizzeria.

3 Put the flour and salt into a bowl, stir in the yeast mixture, then work into a ball with your hands.

Ingredients
Serves 3-4

For the dough:
225 g strong white bread flour
150 ml warm water
15 g dried yeast
1 teaspoon sugar
1 teaspoon salt

For the topping:
1 tablespoon vegetable oil
400 g can chopped tomatoes
100 g *mozzarella* cheese
pinch of salt, pepper and dried oregano

A taste of Italy

4   Put the dough on to a floured work top and knead it for 5 minutes. Roll out the dough into a large round shape. Place on the baking tray and leave in a warm place to rise, while you prepare the topping.

5   Drain the juice from the tomatoes and grate the *mozzarella* cheese. Brush the top of the *pizza* dough with oil, spread over the tomatoes, cover with cheese and season with salt, pepper and oregano. Leave to rise for another 15 minutes.

6   Bake in the oven for 20 minutes. Cut into slices and serve hot or cold.

Always be careful with a hot oven. Ask an adult to help you.

Glossary

Alps A range of high mountains in Europe which spreads through south-eastern France, Switzerland, northern Italy and Austria.

Buffalo A large animal, related to cattle, with curved horns.

Cereal Any of several different plants grown for their seeds, which can be used for food. For example, wheat, oats and barley are cereals.

Croissants Flaky bread rolls that are eaten for breakfast. They are crescent-shaped (like a new moon).

Diabetes A health problem. People with diabetes have difficulty breaking down sugar in their bodies.

Diet The sort of food a person generally eats.

Dough A sticky paste made from flour and kneaded until it is very elastic. Bread is made from dough.

Game Any wild animals that are hunted for sport.

Grazing land Fields of grass where animals such as cattle and sheep are left to feed.

Imported Brought in from another country.

Knead To make a mixture into a paste by pounding it with the palm of the hand.

Middle Ages A period in Europe from about AD 1000 to the fifteenth century.

Midnight Mass Mass is a church service held by Roman Catholics to remember Jesus Christ's Last Supper before he was put to death. Midnight Mass is a special service held at midnight on Christmas Eve.

Olive groves Small areas planted with olive trees.

Paprika A powder made from dried red peppers and used to flavour food.

Polluted Made very dirty. Polluted land and water can be harmful to people, plants and animals.

Preserving Treating food so that it can be kept for a long time without going off.

Risotto An Italian rice dish.

Roman Catholics Members of the Roman Catholic Church – a branch of the Christian Church – which is headed by the Pope in Rome.

Saffron A bright yellow-coloured spice made from crocus flowers.

45

Salami   Very spicy sausages.
Savoury   Salty or spicy; not sweet.
Seasoning   Salt, pepper and other flavourings used to make food tastier.
Songbirds   Small wild birds, such as blackbirds and thrushes, that are known for their calls. Some Italians trap songbirds to eat.
Spices   Strong-tasting substances that are used to flavour food (for example, ginger and nutmeg). They are often made into powders.
Squid   An animal found in the sea with a long hollow body and tentacles. The body is usually cut into rings and cooked.

Starchy   Containing starch. Starch is a kind of sugar found in certain foods, such as potatoes and rice.
Traditional   Made according to traditions, or customs, that have been passed down over the years, from one generation to another.
Vineyards   Fields where grapes are grown for making into wine.
Whey   A watery liquid that is left over when milk is clotted to make cheese.
Wholemeal   Made from the whole of a grain or seed, including the outside husk. Whole wheat grains are ground up to make wholemeal flour.

Further information

Information Books

We live in Italy by Donna Bailey (Macmillan, 1989)

Italian Food and Drink by E. Biucchi (Wayland, 1986)

Italy by Daphne Butler (Simon and Schuster, 1991)

Italy: The land and its people by Anna Sproule (Macdonald, 1987)

Recipe Books

Italian Regional Cookery by Simonetta Lupi Vada (Ward Lock, 1987)

Italian Vegetarian Cookery by Jack Santa Maria (Century, 1987)

The Food of Italy by Claudia Roden (Chatto & Windus, 1989)

Picture acknowledgements

The publishers would like to thank the following for allowing their photographs to be reproduced: Anthony Blake Photo Library 8 bottom, 22 left, 23, 26 bottom, 29 bottom, 32, 38; Cephas 6 right (M. Rock), 10 both (M. Rock), 12 (R. Beatty), 20, 21 top, 24 (M. Rock), 25 bottom (M. Rock), 26 top, 28 both (M. Rock); E. T. Archive 8 top; Eye Ubiquitous 11, 14 top, 30 (all P. Seheult); Hutchison Library 19, 22 right; Isabel Lilley 13 top, 35; Tony Stone Worldwide cover (main picture), 4 bottom, 6 left (J. Cornish), 7 bottom (N. DeVore), 37 (J. Jackson); Topham 9, 17 bottom, 40; Wayland Picture Library cover (inset picture), frontispiece, 13 bottom, 21 bottom, 43, 25 top; Zefa 4 top, 7 top, 14 bottom, 16, 17 top, 18, 27 top, 27 bottom, 29 top (W. Mahl), 31 (R. Bond), 34, 42.

The map artwork on page 5 was supplied by Peter Bull. The recipe artwork on pages 18-19 and 32-44 was supplied by Judy Stevens.

Index